When I

Lada Kratky

Photographs by
Fernando and Barbara Batista

HAMPTON-BROWN BOOKS
MANY CULTURES, MANY LANGUAGES...MANY POSSIBILITIES!™

When I grow up,

want to be a police officer.

Me, too.

When I
grow up,

I want to be an astronaut.

Me, too.

When I grow up,

I want to be a football player.

Not me!

... makes. They are ea...

...through high, tall grass...

...furrows. When I was...

...mes, I failed, but today I...

...lowing; he sets his patterned...

...follow him. Now having...

...I watch myself. I walk...

...ew ones of my own. God gra...

...for my own son. I shall...

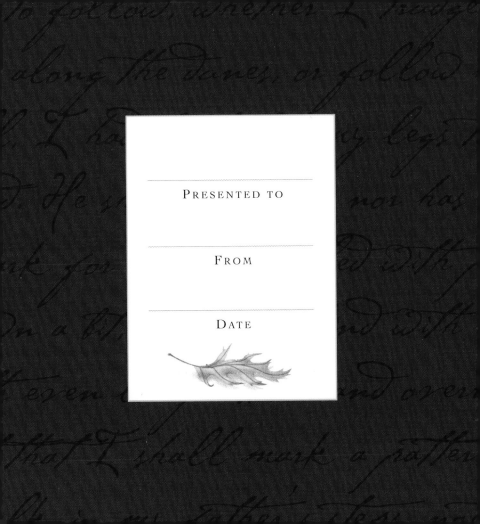

PRESENTED TO

FROM

DATE

Poems
for
Father

A LOVING HERITAGE

WATERCOLORS BY
JO ANNA POEHLMANN

IDEALS PUBLICATIONS, A DIVISION OF GUIDEPOSTS
NASHVILLE, TENNESSEE
WWW.IDEALSPUBLICATIONS.COM

ISBN 0-8249-4110-1

Caseside printed in the U.S.A.
Text printed and bound in Mexico.
Printed by R.R. Donnelley & Sons.

Published by Ideals Publications, a division of Guideposts
535 Metroplex Drive, Suite 250
Nashville, Tennessee 37211

Library of Congress Cataloging-in-Publication Data
          p. cm.
        Poems selected by Elizabeth Bonner Kea. Includes indexes.
        ISBN 0-8249-4110-1 (alk. paper)
        1. Fathers—Poetry. 2. American poetry—20th century. I. Kea, Elizabeth Bonner, 1976–

        PS595.F39 P63 2000
        811'.50803520431—dc21   00–063237

10 8 6 4 2 1 3 5 7 9

POEMS SELECTED BY ELIZABETH BONNER KEA
DESIGNED BY EVE DeGRIE

ACKNOWLEDGMENTS

All possible care has been taken to fully acknowledge the ownership and use of every selection in this book. If any mistakes or omissions have
occurred, they will be corrected in subsequent editions, provided notification is sent to the publisher. COFFIN, ROBERT P. TRISTRAM. "The
Secret Heart" from *The Collected Poems of Robert P. Tristram Coffin*. Copyright © 1935 by Macmillan Publishing Company; copyright renewed
© 1963 by Margaret Coffin Halvosa. Reprinted with the permission of Scribner, a Division of Simon & Schuster. CROWELL, GRACE NOLL.
"The Pictured Father" from *Let the Sun Shine In*. Copyright © 1970. Reprinted with permission of Baker Book House Company. GUEST,
EDGAR A. "Father's Distinction." Used by permission of the author's estate. RICHARDSON, ISLA PASCHAL. "Heritage" from *My Heart Waketh*.
Reprinted by permission of Branden Publishing Company. Our sincere thanks to the following authors whom we were unable to locate:
Anne Campbell for "When Father Sorted Potatoes," Frances Frost for "Father," Strickland Gillilan for "Are You There," John Holmes for
"The Father," and Kathrine Williams for "My Father and I."

CONTENTS

FATHER IS . . .

FATHER

Upon his shoulders weigh the stern demands
Of men and nations; but tall he stands,
   Firm and unfaltering.
A sovereign he, and to no royal hands
   Doth servile tribute bring.

Yet see him bow, one threshold passing o'er
While all his pride's apparel falls before
Young eyes, who greet him, "Father," at the door
   Where love is king.
  — MELVINA GENOA MORRIS

FATHER'S DISTINCTION

A youngster ran to meet him down the street
And took his hand and pattered at his side;
To her alike were victory and defeat;
Nothing to her meant all the marks of pride.

Rich men had passed her and she had not stirred;
A great man in his car had driven by;
Another neared of whom the world had heard,
But on his form she never cast an eye.

And then he turned the corner, and she ran
With eyes aglow and happy beating heart,
To greet with kisses glad the weary man —
Of all the throng to single him apart.

"Proud father you should be," thought I, "and reconciled;
Whatever alien lips in scorn are curled,
Whatever others think, your lovely child
Welcomes you home—the best man in the world."

—EDGAR A. GUEST

YOU SAY YOU LIKE TO FISH

You say you like to fish because you like to fish,
But I know better: in your heart's a wish,
A dreaming wish perhaps, you do not know,
That takes you far where apple blossoms blow
On gnarled old boughs—here the air is sweet
And brook-song magic gurgles at your feet.

You may not know, but every whirring wing
Can make a dreaming echo wake and sing
Within your heart; you like to wade
Deep in the water's cool, sun-dappled shade
And feel the wind as light as a caress,
That soothes your heart to tranquil gentleness.

You like to fish in wind and sun and rain,
And though you may not know it, once again
Old Mother Nature stirs some inner joy
That brings back once again the dreaming boy.

— Ruth B. Field

No One Else

There's no one else that's quite as kind,
Or quite as nice to me;
I've loved him for a long, long time —
His dear philosophy.

He always makes the best of life
Whatever it may bring,
And never fails to lift my heart
Above deep sorrow's sting.

He stands beside me all the while
And smiles when I am glad,
I've loved him for a long, long time —
The man who is my dad.

— HILDA BUTLER FARR

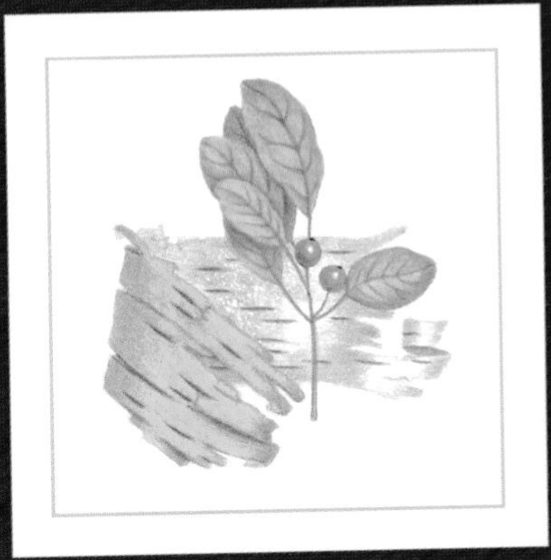

THE AVERAGE MAN

Just a worker at the office,
At the mill, or at the shop;
Cheerful, kind, and sympathetic,
Seeking no excuse to stop.
Plodding, yes, but uncomplaining,
Doing quite the best he can,
Willing to assist his brother —
That's the common, average man.

Not a paragon of virtue,
Has his faults, but how they dim
When you think of all the duties
That the world expects of him.
Meeting endless obligations
That his family may share

Comfort, happiness, and pleasures
Is a heavy load to bear.

He's a hero without laurels,
He's the country's main asset;
He deserves recognition
He would be surprised to get.
For with modesty he labors
As the years fulfill their span,
But to those who know and love him
He's a prince, the average man.
— DELLA ADAMS LEITNER

FATHER IS . . .   15

WHEN IS A FATHER A DAD?

A father's a dad when he builds you a playhouse,
The finest that's ever been built,
Then smiles in amusement to see you prefer
A tent you have made with a quilt.

A father's a dad when he pulls on your pigtail,
Or playfully tugs at your ears;
A father's a dad when he does funny things
To make you laugh right through your tears.

A father's a dad when he says you can help him,
Though he'd really do better alone;
A father's a dad when he fixes your bike
Though he's weary and tired to the bone.

A father's a dad when he guides and protects you,
And all that he has gladly shares;
A father's a father because of your birth,
But a father's a dad cause he cares.

— GLENDA INMAN

FATHERS

The mountain peaks are hidden from view;
They rise so far above the plains,
But sometimes when the day is done,
The setting sun shines through;
And naked then before the world,
They stand revealed for what they are.

And there are people like those peaks,
Who stand above the common herd,
Through storm and stress inviolate—
To them the mountain speaks.
The mountain peaks reach for the stars,
And men who touch them are so few.
— MINNIE KLEMME

FATHER'S LOVE

DAD'S HANDS

Dad's hands are hardened worker's hands,
Unlimited in the tasks that they can do.
They repair bicycle tires, unknot
Tangled fishing lines, or set onions
In long, straight rows with equal ease.
They are gentle hands—cleaning a
Bruised knee, checking a forehead for fever,
Or walking hand in hand with a small child.
Dad's hands are warm hands, filled
With love, filled with dreams, and
Filled with energy to see the dreams come true.
Never completely without the tan of
Summer's sun, these hands are, to me,
The vitality of my world.
—CRAIG E. SATHOFF

PORTRAIT

He comes slowly up the driveway
At dusk on a summer evening —
Tired and weary from the day's work
And over his shoulder he carries a hoe.

A man of the soil all his life,
He's known long hours, hard work,
Worn-out shoes, patched overalls, faded blue shirts,
And sometimes penniless pockets — yet he is rich.

Weather beaten and sun burned face, calloused hands,
Skinned knuckles, sweat-stained brow:
He wears a countenance of strength and deep contentment.
He's battled the elements — sometimes won, sometimes lost —

But always he did the best he could,
Managed to survive and plan the next year's crop.

A quiet, gentle man with a deep love of the soil,
Plants that bloom, sunshine and rain, fragrant hay,

Fat cattle, sleek horses, and white-faced calves—
All their needs before he thinks of his own.
Always ready with a smile, to lend an ear or helping hand,
Solve a problem, fix a toy, to guide and teach, to show the way.

A big dog walks by his side.
A boy and girl run to meet him,
While under the big pine tree, waiting,
Stands a lovely woman.

Finished at last with the day's work
And coming home to supper,
This man with the hoe—
My father.

—DOROTHY MILLER BIRDWELL

FATHER'S LOVE

FATHER'S HANDS

My father's hands are weather-brown —
Sometimes I see them reaching down
To help a little child whose feet
Have stumbled on a rugged street.

Sometimes I see them reaching out
To wrap a woolen cloak about
A traveler chilled with winter rain
Across a midnight-darkened plain.

But often, in the twilight hour,
I see them clasped in humble prayer.
— GRACE V. WATKINS

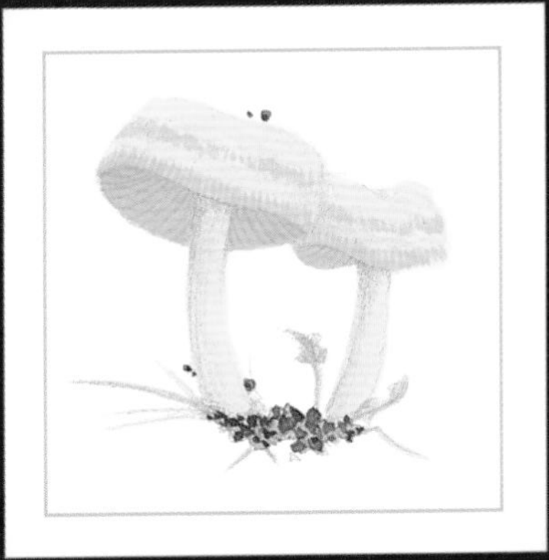

A Father and Son

He towered over me when I was small,
Like some great giant, rugged, high and tall,
Obliterating from me half the skies
Because of his great body, arms, and thighs.

I did not mind; I loved this big, tall man
In all the loving ways a small child can.
And when he swung me up high into space
And pressed me close, and when his beaming face

Was brought close to my own, it was delight;
It was rapture made of joy and fright.
The ground seemed far away, close were the skies,
And heaven's glory shone within his eyes.

Then — I grew up and he seemed to grow down,
For I became the tallest man in town.
I still look up to him from high above,
And the eyes of both of us still show love.

— ROY Z. KEMP

FATHER

My father's face is brown with sun,
His body is tall and limber.
His hands are gentle with beast or child,
And strong as hardwood timber.

My father's eyes are the colors of sky,
Clear blue or gray as rain:

They change with the swinging change of days
While he watches the weather vane.

That galleon, golden upon our barn,
Veers with the world's four winds.
My father, his eyes on the vane,
Knows when to fill our barley bins,

To stack our wood and pile our mows
With redtop and sweet-tossed clover.
He captains our farm that rides the winds,
A keen-eyed brown earth-lover.
— FRANCES FROST

My Father

What have you been to me?
A strong, brown hand that guided baby steps;
An arm that in the evening gloom could show
Strange figures in familiar trees and sky;
A voice that told of famous deeds and men,
That sang old songs to heavy-lidded eyes,
That soothed with words, a childish, aching heart,
While tender fingers bound a gaping wound.
These have you been and more.
When did I ever ask for help in vain?
Or pose some question without a reply?
With you I paced the circle of the stars,
Held converse with the men of ancient Rome,
Beheld the cities long ago destroyed,
And heard the music of your distant land.
—LOUISE D. ROSS

WHAT DAD KNEW

He knew the name of every tree that grew
On homeland hills and by the river bend.
When shy and hidden mayflowers bloomed, he knew
Just where to find them; but he'd then pretend
That small folks on these woodsy expeditions
Had found the fragrant flowers all alone.
He welcomed each wildflower by its name,
The blossoms lost when held in his huge hand.
He loved each furry creature, wild or tame,
And reverenced their Maker and His plan.
The outdoors called him under all conditions,
And growing things he treasured as his own.

He knew the birds and where they built their nests;
He knew and told us how they fed their young.
He loved each season, loved the summer best.
He knew the old songs, loved to hear them sung.

He held the key to childhood, safe and warm,
Was happiest when little folks were near.
He knew just what to do to cure a sting;
His mighty hands could gently do their part
To tend to small, bruised fingers. He could bring
Quick comfort to a childish broken heart.
His mighty arms a bulwark from all harm;
His life, if need be, fortress from all fear.

He knew the streams to fish, could always find
A safe place where young fishermen could stay.
He'd bait their hooks, untangle twisted lines,
Then let them fish the happy hours away.
He'd scorn the whiners and the winners praise
And say 'twas fun to have the kids along!
He knew the ways of love. No ancient knight
Could be more gallant to his lady fair.

continued on next page

He'd proffer wildflowers, berries red and bright,
Wild cherries, or some fern of maidenhair.
And Mom, accepting with a queenly grace,
Caressed the gift and hummed a happy song.

He viewed the distant peaks as feudal kings,
Surveyed their captured lands in ancient days,
For hills and lakes were his. All living things
Were miracles to love and offer praise.
Unorthodox, perhaps, to standard view,
His way of worship of his God above!
He scorned the city ways and city streets;
He liked to call his neighbors by their names
And liked to feel the earth beneath his feet.
He had no thoughts of wealth nor worldly praise.
A lifetime could not teach me what he knew!
I think he learned it in the school of love.

—AGNES M. SLOANE

Are You There

I like to play close to my father's den,
Where he's at work, and every now and then
Ask: "Father, are you there?" He answers back:
"Yes, son." That time I broke my railroad track
All into bits, he stopped his work and came
And wiped my tears, and said, "Boy, boy! Be game!"
And then he showed me how to fix it right,
And I took both my arms and hugged him tight.

Once when I'd asked him if he still was there,
He called me in and rumpled my hair,
And said: "How much alike are you and I!
When I feel just as boys feel when they cry,
I call to our big Father, to make sure
That He is there, my childish dread to cure.
And always, just as I to you, 'Yes, son;'
Our father calls, and all my fret is done!"
— STRICKLAND GILLIAN

MEMORIES
OF
FATHER

THE GOOD YOUNG DAYS

I remember being propped upon one knee
With your large arms encircling me.
Your voice grew so much softer then,
And you were not like other men.

I had to lean way back and look up high
To see the twinkle in your eye
As you sang the songs you loved so well
Of lonely cowboys and the tales they tell.

When your voice joined rhythm with the rocker's squeak,
I settled down, my world complete.
All that a child could want I had
Right then. Yes, I remember Dad.

— ARLENE GROESBECK

FISHING TIME

Out on the blue lake where anglers like to go,
The emerald dragonflies were flitting low;
And father sometimes paused, took time to wish
That he could leave his shop to catch a fish.

The lake was only five short miles away,
Such humid days, dull trading anyway.
Maybe, he thought, it was good to leave his work
To angle in the lake where bluegills lurk.

Ham sandwiches and deviled eggs he'd take,
So good to eat when we had crossed the lake
On summer days when dragonflies would light
Like jewels against the bonnie boat so white.

I'm glad my father fished some summer days
And found his happiness in simple ways;
I'm also glad he never thought it wrong
To take a little fishing girl along.

—GRACE SHATTUCK BAIL

MEMORIES OF FATHER

REMEMBERED DAY

This was a jewel-day from out long years of days,
A shining day, cupped in spring's emerald hand,
When father, with his fishing rods, led me
Through earth's prosaic door to an enchanted land.

I feel again my small hand clasped in his
And match my small steps to his longer stride,
And all my little world is safe and good
As I, with heart in eyes, trudge, loving, by his side.

I see again the shady path we chose,
The leaning tree reflected by the shore;
And gather dog-tooth violets once again and search
To find a fairy ring beneath the sycamore.

I see the sparkling sunshine on the pond,
The dragon-flies pause by the fishing line
Then dart away; and father puffs his pipe.
And all of bursting happiness that day was mine.

— GRACE MAUER

Precious Memory

With fondness I remember
Sitting at my father's knee
While he read a story
Or simply talked with me.
Dad made me feel so special,
For though a busy man,
He would spend those moments
Without another plan
Except to sit beside me,
From all the world apart,
And help me find the answers
I sought with mind and heart.
How precious is the memory
Of Dad calming childish fears
And building a bond between us
That has grown with passing years.

— Lois Anne Williams

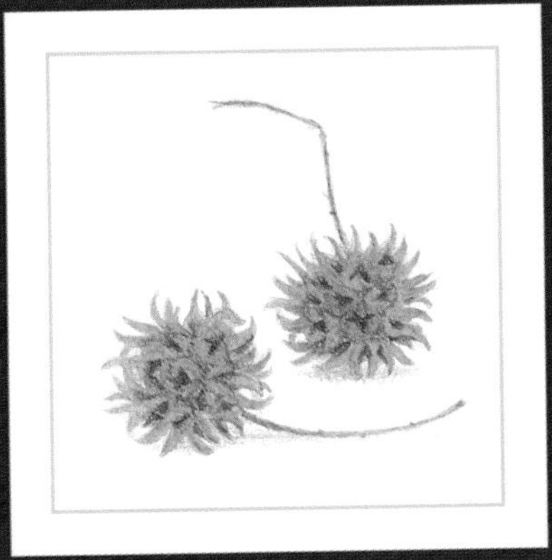

To Dad

You gave me life, you gave me love,
You live in heart and mind,
And in your footsteps I would walk
Slow-trudging on behind.

Yours was my strength, you held my hand,
I basked in your warm smile;
And when you sometimes traveled far,
My heart tagged mile by mile.

You gave me faith; a little child
Found in your kindly gaze
A light to guide through coming years
Down life's uncertain ways.

Although you towered big and tall,
You were just a kiss away,
And often—this was best of all—
You knelt down my size to play.
—RUTH B. FIELD

His Favorite Pastime

Spring had a way of luring him
Along the mountainside,
Where only sounds of waterfalls
And ripples were his guide,
Where bright jeweled waters tumbled
So cool and crystal clear;
My father cast his silver line
In the springtime of the year.

In the shadow of the cedars
And the fir boughs' spreading shade,
He stood where ferns were carpet deep
In the forest's green brocade;
And he watched the wild adventure
Of his fly upon the waves,

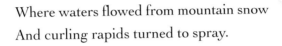

Where waters flowed from mountain snow
And curling rapids turned to spray.

Along the wide, gold-sanded stream,
He fished from pool to pool
And heard the song of waterfalls,
Of ripples clear and cool;
And by the iridescent stream
That tumbled wild and free,
He reveled in his blessed mood
Of joy and peaceful ecstasy.

—JOY BELLE BURGESS

WHEN FATHER SORTED POTATOES

I can remember standing in the gloom,
Holding the light for Father, while he pulled
Potatoes from the sack. The cellar room
Held mystery. The largest ones were culled
For baking. He inspected carefully
This hoarded winter wealth our eyes could see.

The air was crisp. The threat of winter hung
Upon the far-off corners of the moon.
Here the rich scent of jam and pickles clung,
And we could smell the garnered spoils of June.
And Father put them in their proper bin.

I was a little girl, and years have flown
Since my hands held the lamp for Father's sight,
But I would give the grown-up joys I own
If I could go back home just for tonight;
And there within the lamplight circle find
My father's smiling eyes, serene and kind.

—ANNE CAMPBELL

THE SECRET HEART

Across the years he could recall
His father one way best of all.
In the stillest hour of night,
The boy awakened to a light.
Half in dreams, he saw his sire
With his great hands full of fire.

The man had struck a match to see
If his son slept peacefully.
He held his palms each side the spark
His love had kindled in the dark.
His two hands were curved apart
In the semblance of a heart.

— ROBERT P. TRISTRAM COFFIN

MEMORY

When sleep produced a troubling dream
And I cried out in fright,
Soon Dad was there to comfort me
In glow of candlelight.

In his strong hands, he held my own
To make sure things were right;
We formed a great companionship
In still and calm of night.

The candleglow most tenderly
Lit up my dad's dear face,
And gone were lines of work and care,
Which day showed on his face.

The time seemed not to matter,
And Dad took his time to see
That I was both secure and warm —
Then eased away from me.

— CRAIG E. SATHOFF

My Father and I

In those days Sabbath mornings
Meant a long, long ride to town,
Something to learn for Sabbath school,
Going up the hills and down.
Whenever I say, "Our Father"
I better understand,
For the memory of a morning
With Father by the hand.

That prayer seemed such a heavy chore
For one small girl; but I
Leaned against Father's shoulder
As the little hills leaned on the sky —
I thought the words more lovely
On the long, long road to town,
Watching the far horizon,
Going up the hills and down.

And I think I said it better
And trusted it more, when I
Leaned against Father's shoulder
As the little hills leaned on the sky.

— KATHERINE H. WILLIAMS

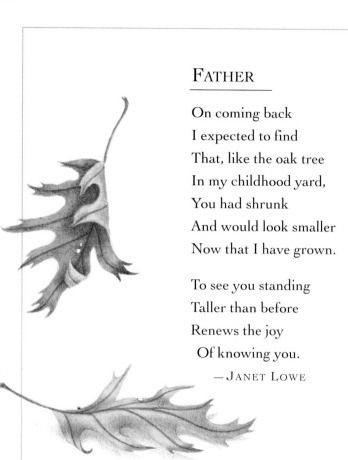

FATHER

On coming back
I expected to find
That, like the oak tree
In my childhood yard,
You had shrunk
And would look smaller
Now that I have grown.

To see you standing
Taller than before
Renews the joy
  Of knowing you.

— JANET LOWE

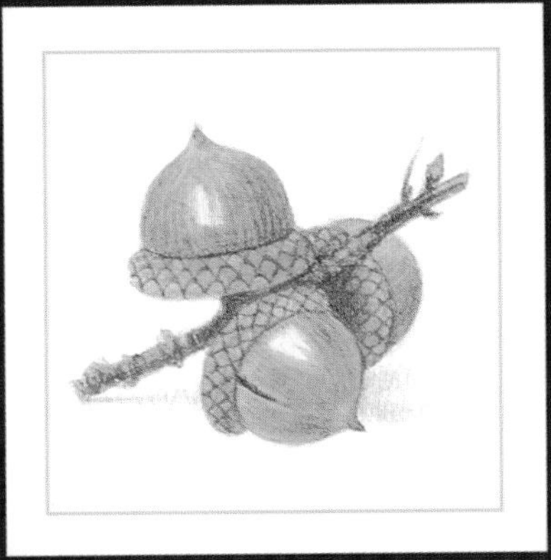

TO MY FATHER

When I was a little girl
And went in fields for walks
And watched you shoveling soil
Or caring for your flocks,
I ran with blowing wind
And felt the warming sun
And jumped along the furrows
And danced 'til day was done.

And when I watched the stars
Reflect the watering streams
And knew that you would care
About my worldly dreams,
I didn't know the dream
Would someday turn toward home
And wish for nothing more
Than fields you made to roam.

—MARILYN NASH HULL

A MAN APART

There was a field, well-fenced with wooden rail,
Where in the spring the lark and oft the quail
Would mark my steps as down the track I came
To bring my father water in a pail.
There I would sit beside the furrow's end
And listen to the train come round the bend.
The while I watched the horses drawing near,
Still pulling strong the rich black earth to tend.

Then we would watch the freight trains rolling by,
Return the wave of trainmen with a sigh,
And dream of cargoes bound from coast to coast,
And follow far the smoke with wistful eye.
My father had adventure in his heart —
The right-of-way was like an open chart —

He spoke of cities far along the line;
I knew by then, he was a man apart.
Like horse and plow, he too was of the land;
The silver rails were not at his command.
He ate his bread with sweat upon his brow;
His feet were chained, but heart and eye oft scanned
The sweep of fields beyond the river's edge.

He knew horizons I had never seen,
Strange ships at sea beyond the sage and sedge.
His hands were gentle with a broken wing;
For him, there was no bird too mean to sing.
The field mouse and the rabbit were his friends —
His soul was freshened by an endless spring.

— MINNIE KLEMME

I DID NOT KNOW

I did not know when I was young
How very much my father cared,
How all the problems of my youth
Were by him wisely, gladly shared.

I did not know, I could not know,
How many thoughtful hours he spent
Planning and praying for my good,
As on my way I blithely went.

The years have passed; a parent now,
I watch my children live and grow;
The love my father gave to me,
At last I know—ah, yes, I know.

—GLADYS DERR BRILL

THE PICTURED FATHER

My father owned wide, fertile fields,
And was grateful for the gain
That came to him from the harvesting
Of his fruit and corn and grain.
He had a passion for the land
Was pleased at its yielding soil;
It mattered not how hard he worked
Nor how intricate the toil.
He would rise at daybreak, seeming glad
To meet the hours ahead,
Feeling he helped the hungry world
By raising wheat for bread.

His arms were strong for any task,
His eyesight clear and keen;
He would wait the usual time of year
To see his land's faint green.
I have watched him stop his plow awhile,
To gaze at the promising sod,
And knowing my father, I knew he was
Praising and thanking God.

—GRACE NOLL CROWELL

REMEMBERING FATHER

Dear Father, I remember
How much you had to do,
Across the years out on the farm,
From sun-up all day through.
The horses must be harnessed
And feed brought for herd and flock,
The wind-pump started, milking done;
And when the big, hall clock
Struck half-past five, you bowed your head
To thank God for our food,
And asked that he might bless
Each one with something rich and good.

You always kept us busy,
Yet we shared a lot of fun;
You never were too busy
For a moment with your son.
The blessing which you asked for us
You gave because we had
The love and understanding
Of a most delightful dad.
—D. A. HOOVER

FATHER'S LEGACY

HERITAGE

One gave his child vast riches—spent his life
In hoarding it. His child, love-starved, grew old
In search of joy, desired and vaguely missed,
In search of something never bought with gold.

Another gave his child companionship.
Taught him content and laughter; love of skies
And fields; the joy of being kind. His child
Knew not that he was poor in others' eyes.

One gave his child vast gold—and left him poor.
"Rank poverty or wealth in each heart lies."
This was the other's priceless legacy.
Both loved—but one was blind, and one was wise.

—ISLA PASCHAL RICHARDSON

PATTERNED WAYS

I shall walk in my father's steps,
Not because it is easy,
But because I like the deep marks
He always makes. They are easy to follow,
Whether I trudge behind him in the snow,
Through high, tall grasses along the dunes,
Or follow him through his ploughed furrows.

When I was small, I had to stretch
My legs to match his stride.
Sometimes I failed,
But always I tried.

He shows no sign, nor has he ever shown a sign,
He is aware of this, my following;
He sets his patterned mark for me
And filled with pride, I bravely follow him.

Now having grown a bit,
I tread behind
With ease. Occasionally,
Unless I watch myself,
I walk with even longer stride
And overreach his tracks,
Make new ones of my own.

God grant that I shall mark a patterned way
As clear for my own son.

—ROY Z. KEMP

Tribute to a Farm Dad

I wish that you could know a man
Who views a greening, plush farmland
And sense the feeling that he knows
Of tasseling corn in long, straight rows.
He sees the same corn reappear
In countless hills, from year to year,
Yet never do I cease to trace
A hint of awe upon his face.
His skin is tinged a red earth tone
Where fifty summer suns have shone
And underneath his straw hat's brim
Are hazel eyes and stalwart chin.
Sinewy hands and arms so strong
From sending bales of hay headlong
Have succumbed to a gentler task

And cradled up a newborn calf.
Another day, another night,
He heads toward shining farmhouse lights
And softly breathes a thankful prayer
For the loving family waiting there.
God, bless this farm dad all his days
That we, his children, might convey
The welling sense of pride we've known
From such a fine example shown.
—LINDA C. ROBINSON

THE FATHER

Hearing his son and daughter
Laugh and talk of dances, theatres,
Of their school and friends
And books,
Taking it all for granted—
He sighs a bit,
Remembering wistfully
A certain mill-town
And his boyhood there
And puts his arm
Across his son's broad shoulder,
Silently as fathers do.
—JOHN HOLMES

A FATHER'S WISDOM

Remember how, when I was very young,
I stood beside you, Father, in the shop,
While busily you pursued a work you loved,
And I plied you with words I couldn't stop?
My questions often trivial to you,
When I asked them in the small alcove,
Were always answered gravely, thoughtfully,
Tempered with wisdom and a father's love.
I gained a wealth of knowledge at your side,
For as you carefully helped me with the wood
You also offered me a set of rules
And guideposts for the road to adulthood.

"You always make a plan," I heard you say,
"Know what you are going to do before you start,
Then try to do the very best you can,
Give to it all your mind, your strength, your heart.
Finish it carefully, make rough spots smooth,
Strike each nail squarely, drive them straight and true,
So you can always know you've done your best
And sense the pride of full achievement too."

I don't think you only spoke of wood,
Spoke only of the job at hand to do;
I was so very young—you could not see
You pointed out a way of life for me.

—EMMA S. McLAUGLIN

FATHER'S DAY

There are little eyes upon you,
And they're watching night and day;
There are little ears that quickly
Take in every word you say.
There are little hands all eager
To do everything you do,
And little children dreaming
Of the day they'll be like you.

You're the little children's idol . . .
You're the wisest of the wise.
In their little minds about you
No suspicions ever rise.

They're wide-eyed little children,
Who believe you're always right;
And their ears are always open
And they watch you day and night.

You are setting an example
Everyday in all you do.
For the children who are waiting
To grow up to be like you.

— AUTHOR UNKNOWN

ONCE

My father stopped us beside a tree
That we might watch the quail hen lead
Her young across our path.

"Once in a while you'll see a sight like this,
Back from the road where not so many pass,"
He said.

A quiet man, alert to whispering earth,
Aware of truth scrawled here and there
By nature in its careful hand.

"Once in a while you'll see a man like that,
Back from the road where not so many pass."
— GERALDINE FEIGHNY

His Special Place

We may not shower him with praise
Nor mention his name in song,
And sometimes it seems that we forget
The joy he spreads as he goes along,
But it doesn't mean that we don't know
The wonderful role that he has had.
And away down deep in every heart
There's a place that is just for Dad.

— Author Unknown

TITLE INDEX

First Line Index

Author Index